curious about

HERDING DOGS

BY CARI MEISTER

AMICUS LEARNING

What are you

curious about?

CHAPTER THREE

3

Farm Life Partners

Curious About is published by
Amicus Learning, an imprint of Amicus
P.O. Box 227, Mankato, MN 56002
www.amicuspublishing.us

Editor: Ana Brauer
Series Designer: Kathleen Petelinsek
Book Designer and Photo Researcher: Sara Hood

Cataloging-in-Publication data is available
from the Library of Congress.
Library Binding ISBN: 9798892008549
Paperback ISBN: 9798892009201
eBook ISBN: 9798892009867
LCCN: 2025012829

Photo Credits: Alamy Stock Photo/David Bagnall, cover, 1, David Gowans, 11, Paulette Sinclair, 5, Tierfotoagentur / S. Starick, 2, 14–15; Dreamstime/Flowersofsunny, 10; Getty Images/ AscentXmedia, 17 (bottom), Dmitriy Kostylev, 2, 6, Grant Faint, 17 (top), Grant Reaburn, 8–9, meegan zimmerman, 3, 18–19, Mordolff, 12, orhankose / 500px, 21; Shutterstock/E LLL, 7 (bottom), Eric Isselee, 7 (top), 7 (second from top), Tanya Consaul Photography, 7 (middle), TrapezaStudio, 7 (second from bottom); The Noun Project/Amir Ali, 13, LOKAL, 22, 23

CHAPTER ONE

What is a herding dog?

A **herding** dog is a four-legged farmer! It helps move sheep, cattle, or other animals from place to place. It keeps its herd safe by keeping the animals in a group. It also protects the herd from wolves and other wild animals.

Herding dogs help keep animals like sheep in the right place.

How does a herding dog move animals to a new place?

Welsh Corgis race around sheep to keep them together.

The dog sends signals to the herd. These signals can vary. Each **breed** has its own style. Border collies like to stare at sheep to make them move. Australian Cattle Dogs nip at the heels of cows to get them going.

BORDER COLLIE

AUSTRALIAN SHEPHERD

GERMAN SHEPHERD

WELSH CORGI

AUSTRALIAN CATTLE DOG

What animals do the dogs herd?

Mostly sheep and cattle. But herding dogs are also used to move goats and reindeer. They can be helpful with ducks and geese, too. Sometimes these smart dogs even try to herd kids and other pets at home!

DID YOU KNOW?
A herding dog can control hundreds of sheep at once!

COMMON HERDS

Herding dogs are trained to move sheep and other animals.

CHAPTER TWO

When does a herding dog start training?

A dog can start learning when it is a puppy. It can watch another dog work. Its **handler** can bring it around the animals it will herd. This helps get the dog used to the animals' sounds, smells, and movements. By six months old, a dog can start practicing herding animals.

Herding dogs usually work in teams on farms.

How do herding dogs learn commands?

Handlers give commands using words, whistles, or hand signals.

Training starts with "come" and "stop." Then dogs learn herding words. "Away" means go left around the herd. "Come by" means go right. "Walk up" means move toward the herd. The handler may also use a whistle. Each whistle sound means something different.

HERDING WORDS

"Cast" or "Flank" = gather herd together

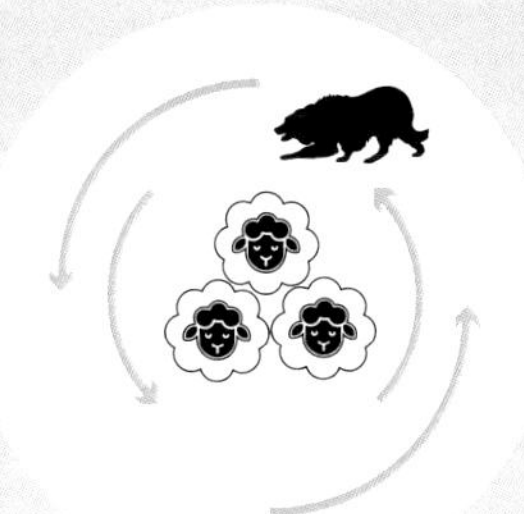

"Away" = go left

"Come by" = go right

DID YOU KNOW?

Most herding dogs can learn 50 or more commands!

What are the first things herding dogs learn?

First, dogs learn to jog around the herd. This is called **outrunning**. Dogs also practice staying quiet and moving slowly. Running and barking too much may scare the animals! Dogs must also learn to lie down when told.

DID YOU KNOW?
Border collies are super speedy! They can run up to 30 miles (48 kilometers) an hour!

This dog runs around the herd to keep the sheep together.

How do herding dogs know where to move animals?

Dogs learn to bring animals to their handler. This is called **gathering**. They also learn to push animals away. This is called **driving**. Smart dogs can move animals through gates or into barns. They practice every day until they get it right.

DID YOU KNOW?
A Welsh Corgi is so short, it can duck under cow kicks.

Many herding dogs compete at county fairs to show their skills.

During competitions, herding dogs race to see how fast they move the sheep.

Where do herding dogs live?

Most herding dogs live on farms or **ranches**. They stay close to the animals they work with. At night, they sleep in the house or in a special barn area. When they're not working, they love to play with their families just like other pet dogs.

Herding dogs may play fetch for fun when they're done working.

HARD WORKERS

One herding dog can do the work of five people on a farm.

How long do herding dogs work each day?

Every day is different! Some days they work from early morning until sunset. Other days they work much less. It depends on when the animals need to move. A herding dog learns when to work and when to rest.

A herding dog's workday changes with the animals' needs.

ASK MORE QUESTIONS

Do herding dogs have any health issues?

How do ranch dogs protect sheep from wolves?

Try a BIG QUESTION: How have herding dogs changed farming over time?

SEARCH FOR ANSWERS

Search the library catalog or the Internet.
A librarian, teacher, or parent can help you.

Using Keywords
Find the looking glass.

Keywords are the most important words in your question.

?

If you want to know about:

- herding dogs and health issues, type: HERDING DOGS HEALTH ISSUES
- dogs protecting farm animals, type: LIVESTOCK GUARDIAN DOGS

LEARN MORE

FIND GOOD SOURCES

Here are some good, safe sources you can use in your research.
Your librarian can help you find more.

Books

Herding Dogs
by Marie Pearson, 2023.

Herding Dogs
by Sara Green, 2021.

Internet Sites

AKC: Herding Group
https://www.akc.org/dog-breeds/herding/
This site gives information about many different breeds of herding dogs.

Britannica: Herding Dogs
https://www.britannica.com/animal/herding-dog
This site provides information about herding dog breeds and the different techniques the dogs use to move animals.

Every effort has been made to ensure that these websites are appropriate for children. However, because of the nature of the Internet, it is impossible to guarantee that these sites will remain active indefinitely or that their contents will not be altered.

SHARE AND TAKE ACTION

Visit a county fair or sheepdog trial to watch a herding dog work.
In a sheepdog trial, dogs compete in how well they herd animals.

Make a model farm with toy animals.
Then draw a map showing how herding dogs move animals from one place to another.

Create a poster about different herding breeds.
Share it with your friends and family.

GLOSSARY

breed A certain type of animal or plant.

driving When a herding dog pushes an animal away.

gathering When a dog brings its herd to the handler.

handler A person who trains and takes care of a working dog.

herd To gather and move animals or people into a group.

outrunning When a herding dog walks or jogs around the herd.

ranch A large farm where cattle or sheep are raised.

INDEX

About the Author

Cari Meister has written many books for children about dogs. She recently rescued a Great Dane puppy from an animal shelter. Cari loves learning about how dogs help keep communities safe. She lives in Vail, Colorado, and sees avalanche dogs at work all winter long.